WOMAN WITH A FAN

WOMAN WITH A FAN

ON MARÍA BLANCHARD

POEMS BY

DIANE KENDIG

SHANTI ARTS PUBLISHING
BRUNSWICK, MAINE

WOMAN WITH A FAN

ON MARÍA BLANCHARD

Published by Shanti Arts Publishing

Interior and cover design by Shanti Arts Designs

Shanti Arts LLC | 193 Hillside Road
Brunswick, Maine 04011 | shantiarts.com

Printed in the United States of America

ISBN: 978-1-951651-85-5 (softcover)

Library of Congress Control Number: 2021940220

Because the best who can, also teach,
as did María Blanchard,
who taught her students, "Go further,"
this book is dedicated to my teachers
who taught me to go further.

I have come here not as critic nor as connoisseur of the work of María Blanchard. I am here as a friend of a shade . . . who has spoken to me through some mouths and some cloudless landscapes.

—Federico García Lorca

Contents

Acknowledgments

Ekphrasis: "María Blanchard's The Ice Cream Cart"

Ekphrastic Review: "María Blanchard's Two Sisters"

Italian Americana: Cultural and Historical Review: "María Blanchard's Portrait of Regina Barahona"

Kaleidoscope: "María Blanchard's Mother"

Masque and Spectacle: "María Blanchard's Woman with a Fan"

Pink Panther Magazine: "María Blanchard's Behave Yourself—Joan of Arc" (as "Abstracted")

Wordgathering: "Speaking of María Blanchard" (the poem), "Bodegones: Her Studio at Last" (as "The Last Weeks in Her Studio"), "Speaking of María Blanchard" (the essay), "Setting the Record Straight on Curvature of the Spine," and "Speaking Even More of María Blanchard"

"María and Diego 1914" (as "Marie Blanchard 1914") appears in *Letters to the World: Poems from the WOM-PO LISTSERV,* edited by Moira Richards, Rosemary Starace, and Lesley Wheeler (Red Hen Press, 2008).

"María Blanchard's Oriental Caprice" (as "María Blanchard's Capricho Oriental") was commissioned by Robin Johnson for a recording in *The New Place Podcast Project.*

"María Blanchard's The Ice Cream Cart" appears in *Ice Cream Poems: Reflections on Life with Ice Cream*, edited by Patricia Fargnoli (World Enough Writers, 2017).

"María Blanchard's Three Portraits" appears in *Veils, Halos, and Shackles: International Poetry on the Oppression and Empowerment of Women*, edited by Charles Adès Fishman and Smita Sahay (Kasva Press, 2016).

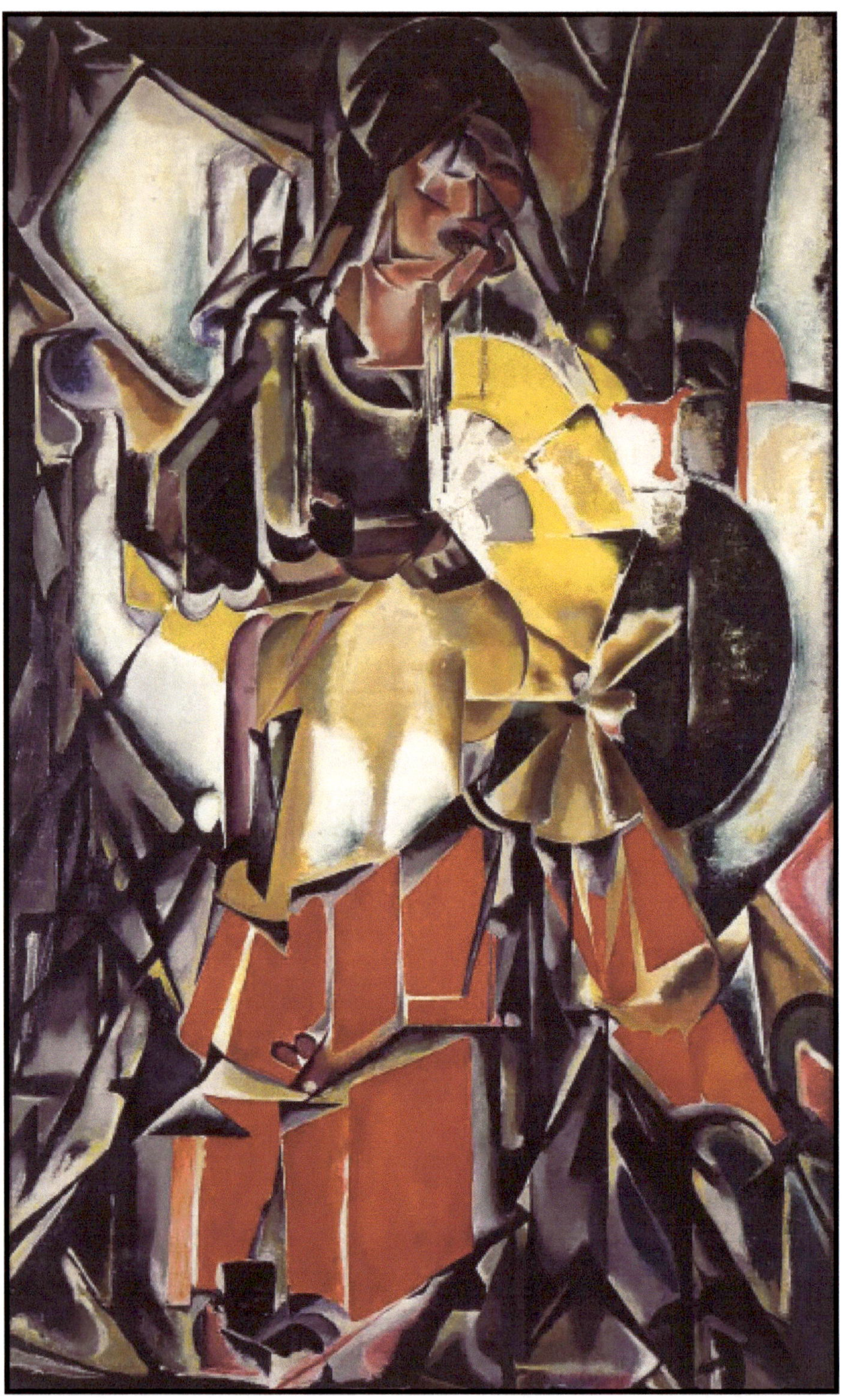

Woman with a Fan

The Reina Sofía Museum, Madrid, Spain

North of here, in the Palace of Catalan Music Hall,
fans froth its matinee audience,
the plain and the lacy, the ones sold to match
the stained-glass windows, tiny mosaics of light
colorful as this painting's big cubist blocks.
The fans could be waves made by women everywhere
except they are Spanish, not the screens of English ladies
nor the large cards stapled to paint sticks sponsored
by local funeral homes and propped up like signs
in the church pews of my American childhood,
where mothers hissed, "Stop. It only makes you hotter."
But grandmothers used them, moved the warm air
with them, and we'd sleep under their wake.
Other than castanets, no prop is so Spanish,
so variable. It's a line that unfolds to a staircase,
a keystone that spreads into an arch—central, womanly.

I found María by way of Lorca's elegy for her,
by way of a footnote in Rivera's biography—by words, then.
Her images, I could not find. For a hundred years
few cared about the art of a woman who bothered
to paint a woman standing with a fan. No matter the artist
fractured her model's dress, spilled voluminous skirts
to the floor as many red books, stacked, scattered,
rising to a gold tablecloth draped at the waist where
her yellow fan opens against her black bodice.

I don't understand how it is that perspective breaks down either,
but I see she is breaking it down, as Picasso broke down
the prostitutes, Rivera broke down an architect. She had vision, but no
pyrotechnics, and she needed them. Though this
might not have been her way, she saw it was a way—
breaking up without breaking down herself,
then splaying, allaying herself till a queen made way
for her a floor above Picasso, next to Rivera,
where we see her work large as theirs for the first time.

Restoration

For María José Salazar and Gloria Crespo

It's happened way before. Hatshepsut,
unnamed by the next Pharaohs' *damnatio*
memoriae so, dislisted from history.
Her two best monuments too,
a pair of red granite obelisks,
felled from her stepson's jealousy
of the heights hers had reached.
It took 3500 years to dig up her reign.

But for cockamamie reasons,
how about Secretary of State
Hillary Clinton photoshopped out
of the photo of the Cabinet watching
the Bin Ladin compound raid
because *Di Tzeitung* editors believe
women shown together with men
might suggest sexuality. Suggestive.

In Blanchard's case, the erasist
probably didn't envy or fear
but had avaricious designs,
we could say, and erasure would tell.
So her rehistorian piled on more paint,
put "Juan Gris" on top, so to speak,
of "María Blanchard," speaking of her,
not erased but blotted out,
daubed over, screwed under.

And while her truth didn't take centuries,
and would out in 80 years, the artist
never knew, just did her work.
Now other women do theirs,
scratch through, scrape at the dab,
let her signature surface,
get her name out there again
by which we all mean—
will you get a look at this?

Portrait of Regina Barahona

Granada, Spain

So many portraits of females,
several gypsies and others, middle-aged,
peer far off or if near, slyly side-eyed;
one elder glances down pensively,
and one other child, turns halfway to show
a bright red hair ribbon she wears.

But *this* girlchild, brought under duress perhaps by mama
to the studio in Carmen del Moro, in "Spain's one city
where life was not seen as a probation for death
but glorious in itself," renowned for the daylight
she sits in, her white cap and dress luminous against
her black curls and teddy bear cradled at her waist,
with her strange aunt smelling of turpentine and linseed oil,

she locks her viewer's eye, not dead
but alive in the eye of us seers
and the artist who has finally located her subject,
the one that she can let full into her gaze, into ours,
the way one can gaze and gaze at the person
that wasn't paid, but brought, the niece, in this case,
here to be seen and utterly beloved.

The Communicant

I saw Picasso's first, of course, because by 1971
even his juvenilia were museumized in Barcelona.
And such juvenilia. I turned to my classmate,
hoping to become cosmopolitan, too, and said,
"Gee, no wonder he invented cubism. He
already knew how to do realism."
The communicant, his sister, kneels in profile,
her tiny body enlarged by white veil and train
yet smaller below the altar and the altar boy
shoulder and head above her on a dais, her father
looming in black, aside him, maybe her mother,
nearly off the canvas, her face mirroring his sister's.

I never knew any First Communion paintings
till Picasso's, but now I can see so many online.
The Italians have centuries of them, often
a gaggle of girls, not one, in white dresses
billowing out into one angelic mass.
In France, Eugène Carrière depicts the girl
swathed in veil and gown ballooning, filling
the center filmily, her misty mind elsewhere,
maybe heaven, against the fuscous background.
Melcher's full-frontal portrait seats the Vermont girl
in a lavender coat over a violet print dress,
stolid, and I wish she could meet Blanchard's,

her girl so sharp mid-canvas, her parted dark hair
streaming outside the veil, flowing along her face:
sharp eyebrows, highlighted eyes, red cheeks.
Her arms open wide like the *Las meninas* ladies.
Her hands clutch a prayer book, dangle an alms purse,
hold high a fancy blue candle. Four pink angels
hover above, an altar rises behind and at left,
scarlet curtains and kneeler drip long gold fringe.
Blanchard, her grant all gone, had had to leave Paris
and settle with her mother on Goya Street in Madrid
to create her Communicant, determined to make her
Spanish. She stands amidst all the symbols in a skirt
short enough to reveal gold boots in mountain pose,
poised to step forward and out some day.

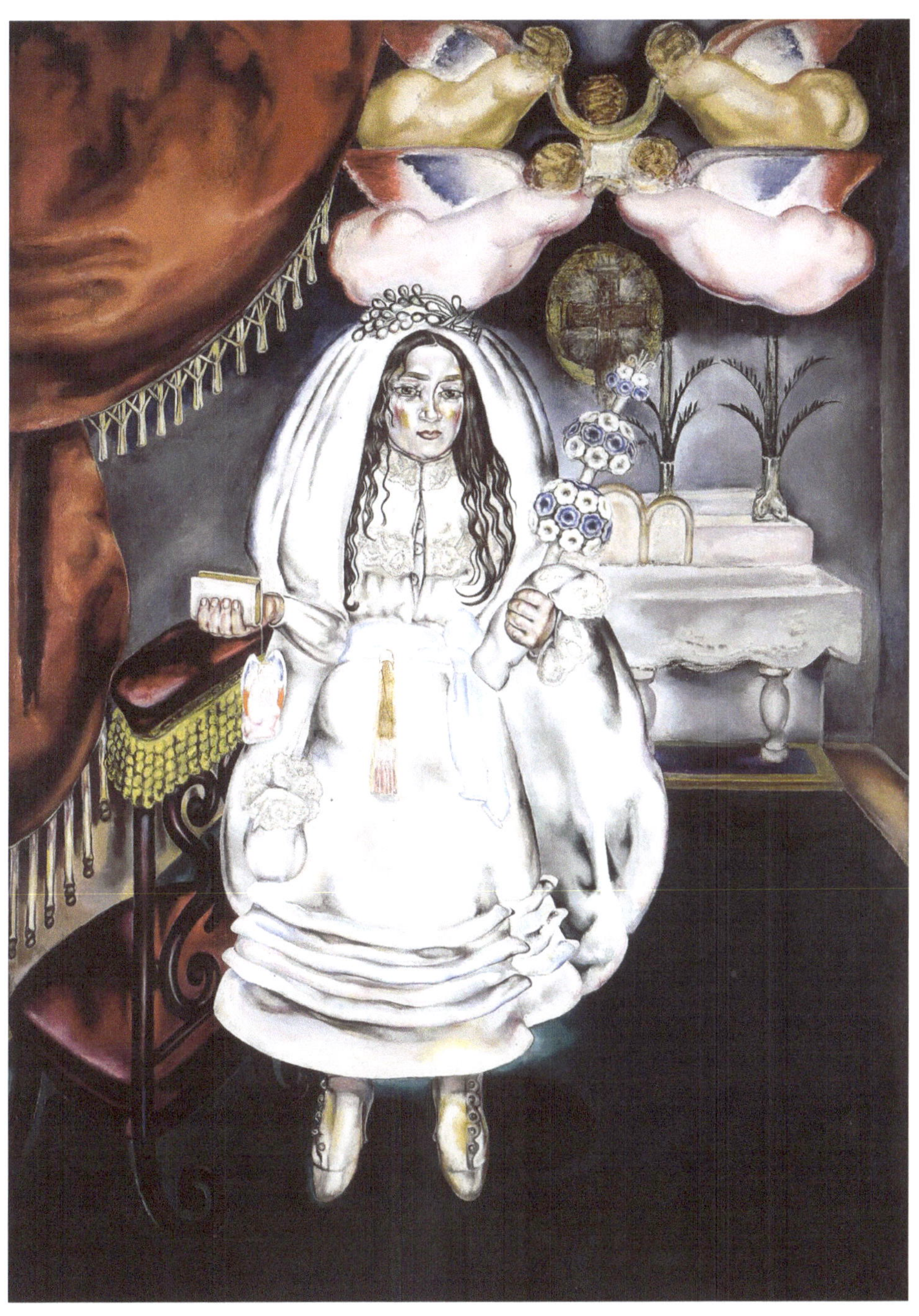

María Blanchard's Mother

Her husband forgot her name, forgot his horse
in the woods of Santander, and, most often, forgot
their daughter, kyphotic from birth from her mother's fall.
The beautiful wife, forgotten, ignored her daughter, too.
Maríe grew smaller and smaller, her head
sinking into her shoulders like a buoy pulled through water,
away from the taunts of the townsmen who thought
touching lottery tickets to a cripple would bring good luck.

"Only in Spain!" she cried, and left for Paris.
She returned with cubism, and turned it in later
for her own vision: the lost, sick, and lonely
in searing colors laid on with a knife,
so stylized her mother even got the point.
Then came the famous, *The Communicant*, then
her last scenes, all mothers and children. A dry search
for God, Lorca said, "no angels, no miracles."

Her refined mother, the legerdemainist
charmed the neighborhood children at her own sickbed.
From under her pillow she'd pull fruit and sparrows.
And keys! How she'd lose them to find them
for the children's amusement: on the armoire,
behind Jaime's ear, in the mouth of the dog.
Over and over, she'd lose, then reproduce them,
trying to prove she hadn't forgotten or lost.

María and Diego 1914

Years later, she laughed about the steak
that came between her and Rivera
in the studio they shared in Paris,
how it weighed raw on the plate,
uncovered for days, a *naturaleza muerta*
that grew more *muerta* each day.
She'd put up with his visions
of man-eating spiders, his stare, too,
at bedposts and lamps; he'd thrown his shoe
at the light bulbs, broken the bathroom mirror
each day. Each day, she'd replace the mirror,
talk him through.
So the steak left to rot
did not symbolize their friendship.
For his part, it was not
a macho matter of cooking exactly.
He had rustled up feasts for many,
filled the table with Mexican dishes once
for Angelina, Apollinaire, and Modigliani.
But Diego would not fry a steak for one woman.
Two weeks passed. The meat, looking
slimy, then green, looked worse.
And María wouldn't ditch the mess, become
just one of the rest of his women, cooking,
cleaning, washing, and cooking more—
though most of his other women were painters.
Why, Angelina's work shrank to miniatures
while she fed his appetites,
the way Frida, two wives later in '32
would drop her brush to walk to his scaffold
carrying a lunch basket covered
with napkins hand-embroidered, "I adore you."
Not María. Not her. She ignored the stench.
But the neighbors couldn't. The twentieth day
they sent the janitor who came and took
plate, steak, and stench away.

Lady with a Fan

When I notice the five women in a London restaurant
all holding fans, I mention María Blanchard's painting
and they smile, say none of them are Spanish, from five
other countries, having met through their daughters,
all of them fan fans, from India, England, Latin America,
ten chic chicks, modern Moms.

In art history, too: so many females with fans
in so many painting by Velázquez, Klimt,
Toussaint, Renoir, Rembrandt, Manet—
And Modigliani's model staring straight on, saying
afterward he'd captured her soul.

Few such studies in America, as though no one flailed them
here, though the hippies sang of them: Dylan
sang "Lady Carlisle" once, and the Dead sang about her
on *Terrapin Station*. And who doesn't love a lady
who tests her two lovers by throwing her fan
in a lion's den to see who'd retrieve it? Isn't it
just like something Jerry Garcia would do?

Blanchard finished "Woman with a Fan," took up
this canvas as another of her old tricks, duplicity
of works, replicas. She slapped the paint on
more roughly, slashed on a black comic smile.
Maybe it's María's little joke: not a woman
this second, distant execution: a lady.

Oriental Caprice

For Robin Johnson

Blanchard's "Oriental Caprice," is called
"singular and curious" among her paintings. Singular
for an artist who believed in multiplicity, reworking
the same theme over and over, maybe never sure if she'd
nailed it. So many treatments of "The Reader,"
the same still life, the girl with a toothache.
You know. How you run lines, hoping out of the running
comes the version that's a take. I know my sister did.
In this case, María got it right right off, the way
we meet a woman and sense a friend for life.

"Lady with a Fan" came later, less spectacular
than the Reina Sofía Museum's "Woman
with a Fan," completed the same year as "Caprice,"
a scene curious for the most Spanish painter
as it's conceived in the Asian mode,
the black scene on the mustard-colored canvas
relieved with some brown, green, red, and least,
some white. We might wonder what possessed her,
and we learn a *friend*: Concha Espina, the one person
supporting, understanding her as her family never did.

A gift for the headboard of Espina's daughter's bed.
What the child must have thought of this picture:
two adults dressed in kimono. sitting in front a low,
sheltering tree, beneath which set an open book,
a cup of tea, some scattered fruit—stand-ins for what
sustains their friendship. And ours? I know my sister
forgot your birth date annually, and so have I
the six times it's been left to me. But not the day,
the celebration of you, my friend, and so
I send this poem three months after the fact.

Cubist Still Life

The Hood Museum, Dartmouth, New Hampshire

It's been in the Hood since 1968,
her only one in the U.S. so far. So far
I didn't know how to look for it
and I still don't know how to look at it
with its dramatically flat simple shapes
in black, tan, brown, cream,
and three shades of gray:
a wide musical note or a water jug?
A wrench on a table
or spoon propped in a knife?

With my bad right eye,
I am not so good at depth perception,
among others, but I see this piece
as a work-out with the guys, what to do
to hang with them, and it worked.
This one has gone out with Picasso
and Braque in exhibits on cubism.
The critics can have it.

When the Great War came,
the first long-range cannon
made just for Paris exploding
on Saint-Gervais, killing eighty-eight,
María focused on humans again—
an old fortune teller reading cards,
children eating lunch,
a man selling newspapers, two women,
one a cook, embracing each other—
In the backgrounds
the flatness she learned here,
abstraction's reckoning. Realism.

Two Sisters

I have a portrait like it, a photo of myself in profile, left arm
slung over my little sister's shoulder. We are ages two and four,
and I'm half naked in the summer grass, she wears a sweet dress.
In Blanchard's painting, the sisters are grown, wearing
long-sleeved floor-length gowns, one red, one green,
both women have the long braids my sister and I were known
for in school. She held onto her hair longer than I,
and I still have the braid she saved before chemo.

"Magnificent in size and color," clearly cubistic
in the underlying shapes of arms and background, but moving
beyond Gris's cubism to her more human faces, especially
the visage of the embraced sister, who looks at us as the other
looks down, this painting holds a story at the left on the table
with its ball of yarn, crossed through with a needle,
and a jar of flowers. Years later, deepest in the penury
she knew all her life in Paris, Blanchard scraped up

the money to buy it back, because, she said, the purchaser, though
a sensitive woman, did not see the sad story that María saw
"on this table that I love." A perfect example of what her grandniece
means when she says in an interview, "María had no business sense
whatsoever."

Behave Yourself—Joan of Arc

Everyone going all abstract   the cubist view opening onto
    rhomboids cones cubes   phonemes graphemes designata
        which is to say form form form
separating separating   act of separation
        properties from their objects
extricating herself
        the failure in Madrid
        the universal family chant
        get a job like your sister Aurelia
(and where was Aurelia's job in 1929 when she moved in with
María in Paris?)
        taking the teaching post in Salamanca—
        But before Madrid had been
            Paris
                had been
            Rivera
                had been
        premios, grants, the artist life
                not
        the uptight university sighing
                not
        the wretched lottery ticket touching

She wrote the letter Aurelia carried in of resignation
resigned   to being the one of the Odd Women
moved with Lipschitz and Gris and their two even women in
        a studio in Beaulieu-Les Loches
set up studies: coffee cup, lamp, fruit, grinder, bottle
broke them up   shattered their past:
her white-dressed *Comulgante*   Gris's silly drawings
built angles and arcs   checkerboards
    holding on to human, keeping color
collage of green wallpaper, slash of ivory antimacassar,
                maroonic people

LETTERS:
P r e s s e Pr e
MGB
Joan of Arc:
rectangles triangles arcs "Sois Sage" quadrant triangles arcs
And other humans
Gris' "Head of Picasso," Picasso so revered by
Gris, the one person Picasso would have willingly wiped
off the Mercator map,
so Pablo could look like Alaska to Brazil
María's women with fans and mandolins, her other musicians,
flat guitars and saxophones.
a tranquil living
separated too from Rivera and his ravings
his all too solid fleshy needy flat-backed women
and his little fleshy heirs she'd babysat
keeping color holding to the human
knuckling down not under, having the upper hand
sovereign, reigning over abstraction.

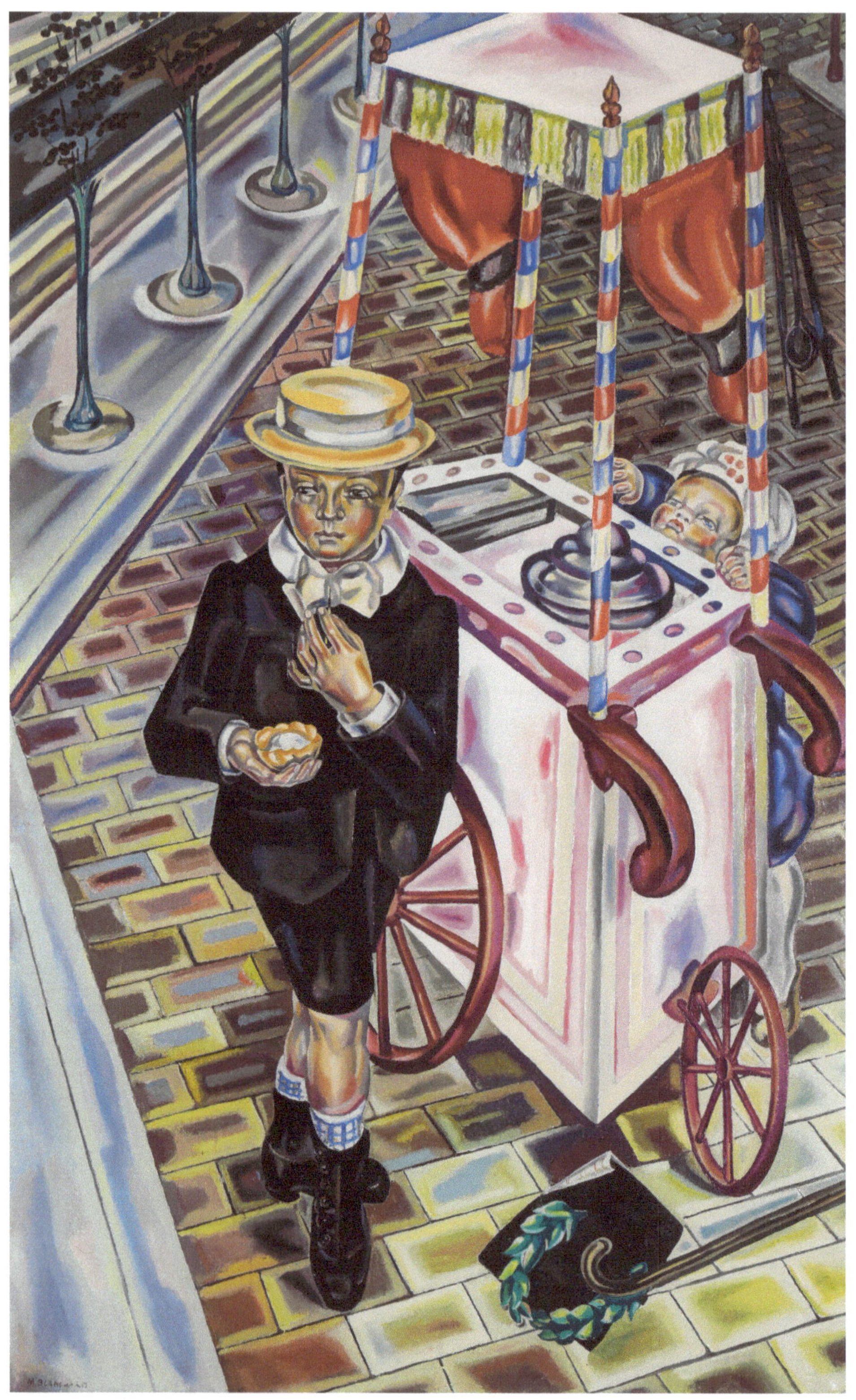

The Ice Cream Cart

I had seen this scene as I was meant to, a certificate
on the ground, the crown thrown on top, the fluffy bow
of his white shirt matching the white band of his boater.
His stiff black jacket, the scalloped bowl of vanilla ice cream.
I tried to see what the critics saw in the angle of his arm
against the paving bricks, the romboidalness of it,
as they say in Spanish. It's not the aesthetics got me.

My friend, a nurse, said, "Look at the girl behind the cart,"
and I do, see how I missed her, barely able to stretch
to hold the ledge of the cart. I remember that reach
to the shelf that held suckers at the bank,
to the bookshelf where the librarian waved for me
to get books myself though I was not tall enough to.
Eventually, they were handed down to me by an aunt
who had *The Scarlet Letter*, whose "A" I could not grasp.

So I don't mean my reach left me with the nothing
that this girl's does. She has arrived after the boy
and has thrown her cane down on top of his laurels,
would like some sweet herself, holds on with one hand
for support, waves her other hand just above the edge,
but it seems the ice cream man
left the picture once he served the boy whose
back's turned on her, eyes staring further off, blasé,
used to such awards, such treatment and treats.

Three Portraits

Her curator calls these "execution of duplication."
Watching her students, she'd sidle up,
say, "C'est fini; n'y touchez plus,"
and if they would protest they weren't finished,
they wanted to improve it, she'd say,
"Then take another canvas and go further
with the same subject."
Not just for beginners, but her own practice,
as in her fourth decade she produced these three
whose differences draw me.

i. Head of a Moor

Against the mustard-colored background of *Capricho*,
her earlier painting, she places this portrait:
a dark olive face and hands, deep gray lines
in the headdress and sleeves,
the asymmetric face, eyes a bit out of kilter.
The hijab seems impossibly wrapped,
pinned at the heart by the woman's two
shovel-shaped hands.

She looks the youngest of the three, barely a teen,
like the little girl at the front of the boat
to Algeciras whom I watched in 1971 while dark men
in heavy robes, despite the heat,
were shoved and shouted to the back:
"Vosotros moros! Pa!"

"How can you say there's no race problem in Spain?"
I asked my hosts. "This is different,"
they answered. "Moors are not like your Negroes.
Moors are dirty and lazy and bad."
María's Moorish girl looks out at us,
as astonished as I was.

ii. Figure of a Girl

Chalk, loose and free, the hijab
now wrapped just right, held on the opposite shoulder,
by hands that looks handier. The eyes still seem off,
the nose and mouth, centered.
She looks older to me, about twenty-one,
and her robes are whiter.
This is the one the critics prefer.

iii. Figure of a Girl / Head of a Moor

Two titles, as though she can't decide,
and the hijab, the same in our time as then.
So France passes "the veil law." I can't decide either.
On my American beach today, a husband
in white short shorts and t-shirt, led his wife,
in long slacks under her long-sleeved dress,
wearing her hijab in the 8 a.m.-already- 90-degree day,
through a series of calisthenics: running
backward, sit-ups in the sand, arm circles in the hot air.
I want to support her right to wear what she wants,
but it's hard to uphold in this heat.

This painting is most stylized, the folds in the robe
as sharp as the angles of Blanchard's many
cubist still lives, curving in counter-position
to the erect face and torso. For all the style,
she moves me most, her straight-on stare
sadder than the second take, and calmer,
the mouth a thick slick of lips with slight downturn,
eyebrows as defined as over-waxed ones today,
the skin much darker, the face most symmetrical,

all very neat and troublesome.
I talk to the woman next to me on the T,
her head wrapped in a hot pink scarf,
laughing with her, and her daughters
complain they can't hear their Kindles
because of our noisiness, and she answers.
"For respect," she says, pointing to her head,
"yes, but not too much," and she motions
over her face as though putting on purdah
and throwing it off: "No, no. Too much."

Execution of Duplication: *Woman with a Fan*

The Reina Sofía Museum, Madrid, Spain

North of here, in the Palace of Catalan Music,
fans froth its matinee audience,
the plain and the lacy, the ones sold to match
the stained-glass windows, tiny mosaics of light
colorful as this painting's big cubist blocks.

The fans could be waves made by women everywhere
except they are Spanish, not the screens of English ladies
nor the large cards stapled to paint sticks sponsored
by local funeral homes and propped up like signs
in the church pews of my American childhood,

where mothers hissed, "Stop. It only makes you hotter."
But grandmothers used them, moved the warm air
with them, and we'd sleep under their wake.
Like castanets, they're a Spanish prop, variable,
a line that unfolds to a staircase, a keystone

supporting an arch—central, womanly.
So many portraits of women through history
lounging, sitting, standing with a fan. But this artist
fractured the model's dress, spilled voluminous skirts
to the floor as red books, stacked, scattered,

rising to a gold tablecloth draped at the waist where
her yellow fan opens against her black bodice.
I don't understand how it is that perspective breaks down either,
but I see she is breaking it down, as Picasso broke down
the prostitutes, Rivera broke down an architect.

Not her invention but she had a vision, no pyrotechnics,
and she needed them. So she splayed, allayed, spread
the woman into as many views as uses for a flabellum,
that liturgical, ornate, plain, pagan, Christian, impractical
instrument. We wake in the breeze of a new millennium.

Resolution

(A Gwawdodyn)

Strangers touched their lottery ticket
to her back, trapped her in their thicket
of folk lore truck that she would bring them luck—
And she? She could like it or lick it.

She'd have none of that, nor anyone's pity
as she packed up and left her home city
and all of Spain for Paris, where, on a terrace
at a party, she met Rivera, handsome and witty.

He found her beautiful in many ways, too:
"A most gorgeous head and hands—but her body? who
could?" quoted his second wife. Duly noted.
For a while the work got her through

the hurt, so she even babysat
for the first wife, but then to hell with that.
María stayed friends to both, to her end,
but never protecting nor protectorate,

painting through, painting through, leaving
behind what didn't feed her seething
need to make her art, these images of her heart
rendered visible for us through all her grieving.

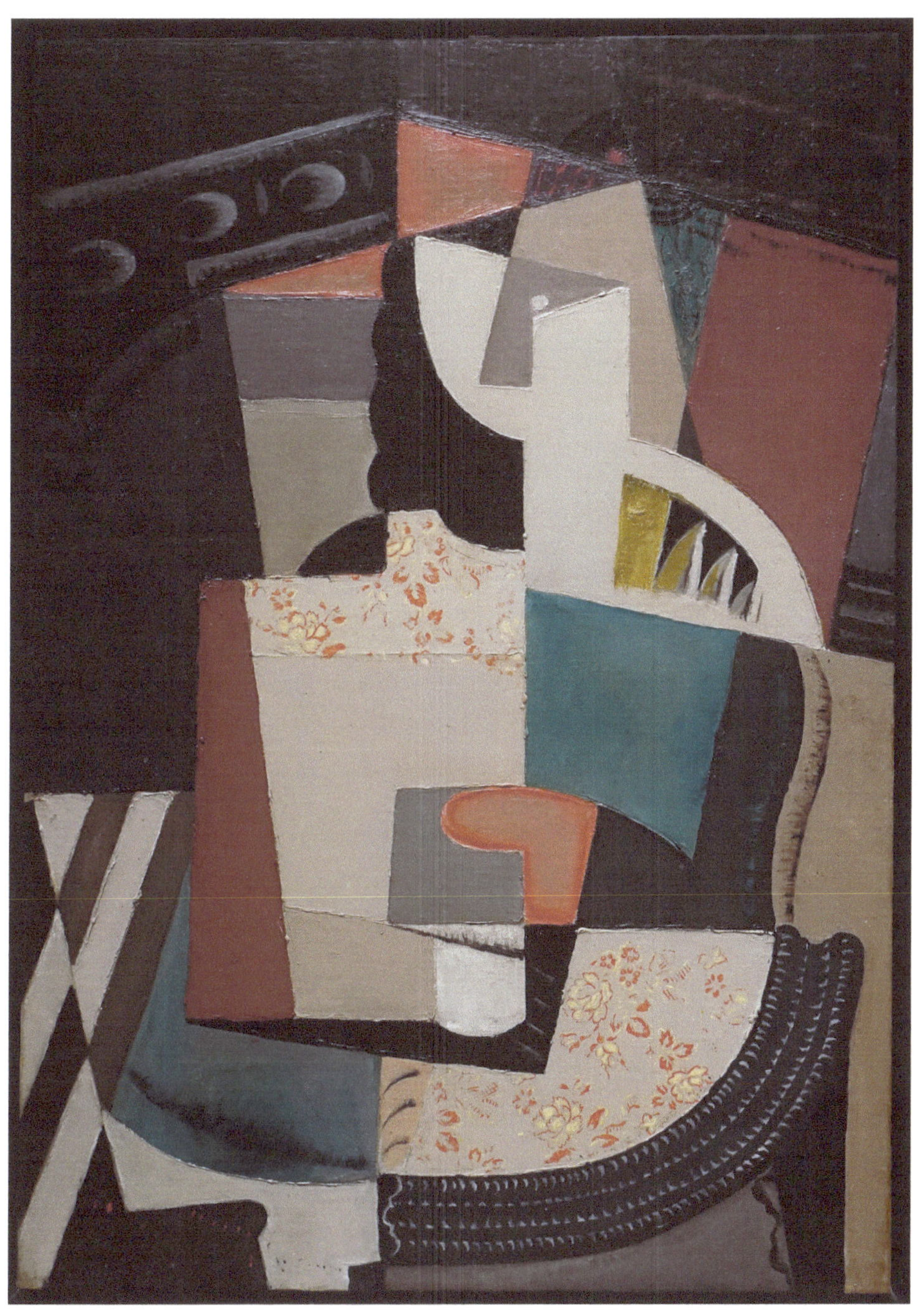

Child with a Handkerchief / Toothache

After Andrew Marvell

With what difficulty
the little girl begins this day,
her head against the pillow; see
her body propped, her chin wrapped
with a white handkerchief, tied at
the top to a spray
        above the knot
like little ears. What you don't see: a cure. It's not.

This was the lot
of 1930's kids: remember *Our Gang*
Comedy's Alfalfa, his sore gum spot
rendered clear to the audience with the cloth
tied round his face, ending in the moth-
wings, bandana-patterned? He sang,
        once healed, off-key,
cured by a vicious tug at the tooth, finally free.

Most 1950's kids were more attended to,
sent to dentists, doctors, and ballet
with regularity, fewer folk cures, less to do
with sitting sadly, like my mother at five
with mastoid, barely alive
when an uncle gave the money to pay
        the hospital bill.
She told the story often; I remember still,

but I didn't that week in '70's Segovia
when I lost a filling to chewing
one of the candies I had bought for the kid
in the family I lived with. So I tripped
down Calle Juan Bravo, skipped
class—what had I been doing
        the prof would ask—
taking myself and my tooth to task.

I entered the office where I'd been sent,
looked for a person to report to
but saw no one who could be the attendant,
just a room of people. "I'm an emergency!
Una emergencia!" Expecting urgency
would follow and they'd resort to
          citing my dire case
and I'd be admitted then, posthaste.

But no, the same silence ensued
that filled the place before I entered.
So I stopped and reviewed
the circle of patients. Each sad swollen soul
clearly had dental pain taking its toll,
each clearly *in extremis*, centered,
          like this child, in piety,
on waiting while her hurting, "the teething anxiety."

I'm back to her as I lean against the padded chair,
in my study. How far art can take us.
Back to this child, then María's pillow, where
she herself rested from the strain of kyphosis,
ignoring poverty, illness, and the neurosis
she endured that would make me
          resign. I try to learn
instead as I head to the end to turn and return.

Speaking of María Blanchard

And to speak of María Blanchard cannot be, should not be, a cold literary exercise. —Paloma Fernández-Quintanilla

i. Lorca' s Eulogy

Between teen face fuzz and the family mirror,
I saw my first painting by her:
a faun and four bathers,
and I thought of a tall María, here

in scarlet, shabby and vulgar as an Amazon.
I took out my little notebook to write upon,
the one all boys carry to open
and inscribe with names of women

they don't know but would like to take
to a room of moss and illuminated snails
in some tall tower or a ship with full sails.
"Wait," they said. "She's a hunchback."

I come today not as critic or connoisseur
I tell you not for truth or falsehood's lure:
María's lifelong search was a dry one,
no miracles, but one of pure earth, pure.

•

"It's not the truth, the stories of her mother's fall from a horse. It may be congenital . . . It may be genetic . . . No one is to blame."
—Dr. José Ramón Rodriguez Altonaga

•

"After Salamanca, never more would she return to Spain. She cut her hair, went back to Paris."
—narrator in *26, Rue du Départ, Érase una vez en París*

•

ii. Obituary in L'Intransigeant

Her work occupied a superior place in contemporary art.
Her powerful painting, made of mysticism
and passionate love of her profession
will remain as one of the most significant
and authentic of our epoch.
Her life as a recluse in illness, on the other hand,
contributed to her unique development
and the sharpness of the most beautiful
intelligence of her time.

•

Her strong character and tough existence earned her the respect of her colleagues, who came to accept her as an equal in an environment culturally dominated by men.

—María José Salazar

•

She was at the heart of that artistic moment [with] a personality all her own.

—Gloria Crespo

•

iii. Maud Sumner, Her Student

"C'est fini, n'y touchez plus,"
she would sometimes say
when I wanted to work longer on a certain canvas.
"Then take another one, and go further
on that, if you can, doing the same subject."

"Tant pis si on est malade,"
as if not sick, she struggled to earn enough.
Matisse, Claudel, and Severini used to come.
Picasso not so much, busy
with his own work. But he was at her funeral.

She was in great pain,
and I could hear her cursing. María
slipped away quietly in my arms.
I still have bits of her furniture. Friends
have said to me, "Why don't you get some nicer?"

I don't always tell them the reason.

Bodegones: Her Studio at Last

"If I live, I am going to paint
many flowers," she said in April.
The Blue Trains were arriving
in Paris on the way to Calais
from the Riviera, full of roses,
violets, and jasmine, clouds
of bright yellow mimosa for sale,
tourists returning home.

After her burial in Bagneux Cemetery,
her casket accompanied by her patron,
her family, and friends, and finally,
the vagabonds and indigents
she had helped for years,

some returned to clear out her studio
filled with canvases, half-prepared,
prepared with a first layer of primer
the canvas threads showing through,
finished paintings, multiple versions
of an earlier work,

and then the works she turned to
toward the end, the bodegones,
that Spanish still life set
in pantries and bars, her quadrants
of cherries, one of grapes, another
of onions. She had long given up
broken planes, fanned out,
and she never got to the flowers
but here stand fleshy, full vegetables
and fruits spread around on plates
and in baskets with napkins and glasses,
waiting for company.

The following three essays were written for *Wordgathering* and are included here to offer some details about the life of María Blanchard that may provide context for the poems.

Afterword: Speaking of María Blanchard

I now know that María Gutierrez Blanchard was born in 1881 in Santander, Spain. Blanchard studied art in Spain, lived and worked awhile in Paris, and returned for a time to Spain where she taught at Salamanca University and exhibited her artwork. Born with a congenital spine disorder, she was left with a hunched back and difficulty walking. Worse, she was plagued by backward Spanish attitudes toward disability. (The poet Federico García Lorca noted the harassment caused by one particular Spanish superstition that it was good luck to touch one's lottery ticket to a crippled person.) Blanchard left Spain to spend the rest of her life teaching, painting, and exhibiting in Paris until her death in 1932 after years of health problems and accompanying pain and penury.

However, I knew little of this when I first saw her name in 1989 while reading a translation of Lorca's prose collection[1] that opens with a eulogy to María Blanchard. I wondered who she was. Lorca said when he came across the first Blanchard painting he had ever seen, he was fascinated by the image, but all that anyone wanted to tell him was that Blanchard was "a hunchback, you know." In the brief, two-page eulogy, Lorca talks about this woman he had never met: her family, her famous artist friends, but most about the struggles she endured because of her physical condition. What intrigued me, though, were his brief references to her painting: "energetic color . . . laid on with a palette knife." Because I had been writing ekphrastic poems on Frida Kahlo's paintings with some success, I wondered if Blanchard might also be an inspiration. I have to feel some connection to the artist or painting to write ekphrastic poems, and I did feel a connection. Both women were short in stature (as am I). Both produced their art despite years of debilitating pain from back problems, Kahlo's from the famous bus accident, Blanchard's from birth. And while I didn't have physical disabilities, my early years in writing were plagued with emotional and mental setbacks. Each of these women provided me with a model of persevering in my art despite personal difficulty.

Yet finding Blanchard's art seemed impossible for me in 1989, off in the hinterlands of western Ohio without means to travel back to Spain. I researched and found a book of Blanchard prints in interlibrary loan, but was crushed when it arrived: a photocopied book with nothing but the blots of black that one got in those pre-color photocopy days. The prints were simply unseeable.

So I began writing poems about what I had of the biography of Blanchard from a few snippets I had found. In addition to Lorca's eulogy, I located (also on interlibrary loan) a brief personal memoir of Blanchard by the South African painter Maud Sumner, who was a student and then an apartment mate. Finally, I found the briefest reference to Blanchard in a footnote of a biography of Diego Rivera, with whom Blanchard once shared a studio. That story just cracked me up.

Out of these fragmentary sources, I drafted three biographical poems. One, a free verse poem, "Maríe Blanchard's Mother," uses facts from the Lorca eulogy, from which I imagined more of the strained relationship between the mother and daughter. In publishing the poem in *Kaleidoscope,*[2] I first encountered the difficulty of how to discuss María Blanchard's disability today. The historical accounts are in Spanish and not necessarily accurate. I continue to struggle, too, with very clinical language on the one hand, which sounds too Latinate in English, and the plain terms that sound disrespectful. So the one definitive art catalogue to date states [my translation]: "María Blanchard suffered from birth a kyphosis, which is to say, a double deviation of the vertebral column with posterior and lateral curvature...with a prominent humpback." In the final publications, I asked input on diction in referring to Blanchard from the journal's editors, who chose the word "kyphotic."

My second biographical poem, "María and Diego 1914" is a narrative poem in rhyme and slant rhyme (every four lines but cast as one long stanza) that retells an amusing (and yet telling) incident about Blanchard and Rivera from their time sharing a studio in Paris. The incident reveals Blanchard's feistiness and her refusal to back down or bow down to Rivera, making her in fact the opposite of the more solicitous Kahlo in her relationship with the famous male. Whereas Kahlo had waited on Rivera like a handmaid, Blanchard was not that kind of woman, despite her love for Rivera. She was my kind of person.

The third biographical poem was titled "Lorca on María Blanchard," a found poem from lines in Lorca's eulogy. For years, it remained a stalled draft until recently when I decided I needed to explore something I hadn't yet realized about Blanchard. I tried adding Maud Sumner's words to Lorca's. Then I came on the line (now the epigraph): "And to speak of María Blanchard cannot be, should not be, a cold literary exercise." In choosing the form of a found poem, did I have a cold, literary exercise? Did I need something warmer? I decided that translating Lorca's original words in Spanish to the slant-rhymed quatrains I used in "Maríe Blanchard 1914" might create something warmer. The result is published in this issue as "Speaking of María Blanchard."

Interestingly enough, the task I set for myself as a translator was not the usual task I have had in the past of trying to express in English a rhyme from another language. In this case, I was trying to express a rhyme in English from a non-rhyme in Spanish, since Lorca was not performing poetry but speaking in prose. Rhyme is almost always a more difficult task in English than in Spanish. However, rhyme in any language tends to be more memorable that non-rhyming language.

Then, too, I thought that some of the 1975 translation phrases seemed to strain today, so "bozo naciente" could be "peach fuzz," but I wanted something more contemporary, which I hope "teen face fuzz" is, while also carrying some assonance and alliteration with "between" and "family" in the same line. I took some liberty by way of addition. The phrase "illuminated snails" is an exact translation of Lorca's "caracoles iluminados," so I allowed myself the invention of "ship with full sails" to rhyme with "snails." The end words "Connoisseur" and "pure" are cognates from the Spanish, one from early in the eulogy, one toward the end, and they made for a useful rhyme with "lure," my own addition.

In preparing for publication, I suddenly remembered some lines from a Colombian folk song set in the city of Cartagena: *Caracoles y corales formarán / Un sender tapizado hasta al mar.* ("Snails and corals form a tapestry path to the sea.") I was struck with translator's guilt (i.e., the sin of omission) by the sudden memory of the Colombian who told me that "caracoles" in this song refer to the snail-shaped streetlamps in that Colonial city. Was Lorca speaking literally here, of carrying a woman up to his room illuminated by streetlamps? Or was that definition a Latin American regionalism he would never know? I wrote fellow translator Don Cellini, who compounded the problem by pointing out that the word "caracol," in addition to meaning "snail" and "streetlamp," was also the word for a winding staircase, not to mention an Andalusian poetry form. (And Lorca was Andalusian!) I have decided to leave the word as "snails," but here I turn them over to your imagination to see mollusks, street lamps, stairs, or poems in that line.

As a translator, I recognize that the first half of this poem involves some invention that I would not allow myself in a pure translation. However, as a poet and a student of Lorca, I feel this poem conveys how he thought of and spoke of María, and how Maud Sumner thought and spoke of her: not coldly, but as two friends, one she'd never met, the other a dear companion, both of whom deeply admired her passionate life and work.

Then, in 2008, I finally achieved a decades-long dream of returning to Spain, where I had studied for a semester in 1971. My second day, in Madrid, in the very new Reina Sofía Museum, I stumbled upon the first Blanchard painting I had ever seen, *Woman with a Fan*, a huge, amazing painting, which hangs next to a Rivera painting and a floor above Picasso's *Guernica*. Hers is a tremendous work, very female, very Spanish, very cubist, and wholly María Blanchard. While I was at the museum, I found a 2004 book: *María Blanchard: Catalogo Razonado, 1889-1932,* containing all of Blanchard's available works, the first comprehensive treatment of her work.[3] I brought a copy of the book home, where I have been composing poems about her paintings ever since.

Whenever I google her name, which I do regularly, I find more references to Blanchard; a college has begun to collect and show her paintings, and several of her paintings are newly up for sale in galleries. Meanwhile, in a Temple University Disability Study blog, someone recently asked if anyone has explored her work from a disability history perspective. There is no answer, but I believe there will be one someday. Blanchard's Wikipedia biography is now available in English as well as Spanish, and it is accompanied by a photo of Blanchard, standing in the shadows giving an art lesson to a female student who is herself seated in a wheelchair. Perhaps just by being María Blanchard, she is giving a second lesson from her position, a lesson in getting the work done, despite disability and pain, despite poverty, despite gender and the lack of critical acclaim. Despite all that, an artist finally is not necessarily the one with wealth or health or fame: she is the one who creates art.

---

1. "Elegía a María Blanchard," now in the public domain, appears many places online. The translation referred to here (in addition to my own) is that of Christopher Maurer in *Deep Song and Other Prose,* by Federico Garcia Lorca, edited and translated by Christopher Maurer, New Directions, 1980.

2. *Kaleidoscope: Exploring the Experience of Disability through Literature and the Fine Arts:* Issue 58, "Reflections on Disability and Childhood."

3. *María Blanchard: Catalogo Razonado: Pintura 1889-1932*, edited by María José Salazar, Museo Nacional Centro de Arte Reina Sofía, 2004.

Setting the Record Straight about Curvature of the Spine

When I settled in to watch *26, Rue du Départ*, a documentary on María Blanchard, I was struck by its forthright discussion of Blanchard's physical condition. For example, Diego Rivera's daughter, Guadalupe Rivera, goes on at length about how the relationship between her father and Blanchard was complicated by Blanchard's appearance. Regarding the stories about the causes of her disability, I was glad to hear Dr. José Ramon Rodriguez Altonaga say, "No es la verdad . . . [It's not true . . .]." These things may be caused by a variety of factors, he says. It may be congenital, genetic, but no one is to blame.

I myself, much to my own chagrin, had repeated in one of my first published poems about Blanchard the story that María's disability came from her mother's fall from a horse. I had read the story in an elegy that Lorca had written and delivered, and I passed it on when I found it over and over in recent online biographies of Blanchard. Then on Facebook, my friend Maria Bonnett questioned the outdated story. She posted:

> I am curious about her disabilities, though. It was said that María sustained her injuries when her mother fell while she was pregnant with her. I suspect that wasn't her true diagnosis. Fetal injuries are rare in cases of falls or even car accidents for that matter. Her deformity appears to be more suggestive of *osteogenesis imperfecta*, or brittle bone disease. Not much was known about this disorder in the early 1900s. At that time, most congenital malformations were blamed on something the mother did during her pregnancy. I hope more research will lead to the discovery of her true illness.

Suddenly, I was struck, recalling my very first psychology class in college, which was the first college lecture class I took. The professor introduced the subject of autism, reviewing the literature on what the causes had been attributed to previously, beginning with the earliest, when the cause was determined to be mothers who were cold, unfeeling. He quickly dispensed with that as not the cause and moved on to more modern analyses, ending with, as I recall, "Well, we don't know." I learned then and often after that when we don't know, we blame the mother.

Bonnett is a retired nurse practitioner who spent a big chunk of her life birthing babies as a midwife, so she is not only curious about these things, she knows a lot about them. And she has always appreciated art. She told me that after I posted on Blanchard, she spent the afternoon looking at the Blanchard images online. I asked her what term one should use in discussing María's disability. I had used kyphosis, since some people feel that "hunchback" is disrespectful. But every time I used "kyphosis," readers asked, "What's kyphosis?" Bonnett replied:

> Kyphosis is a medical term that defines the outward curvature of the thoracic spine. It is a symptom one sees upon exam, not the disease itself. "Hunchback" is the common term. There are dozens of medical disorders that can cause kyphosis, some genetic, some congenital. Genetic causes stem from improper DNA sequences that result in the spinal deformity. Congenital defects are caused by improper formation during embryo development.... María presents with a "constellation" of medical problems. Not only did she have kyphosis, she also had hip dysplasia that limited her ambulation. She was also considered a dwarf, or short stature. This is more in line with a genetic problem with her bones, like *osteogenesis imperfecta*. But since she never had a true diagnosis, it is just my educated guess. Most children born with OI have a triangular-shaped face, and her painting is the best clue that that is what she had. Look at her self-portrait when she was younger; her face is in the shape of a triangle!

> Her mother was probably cold and distant, and I don't think I would blame her. Her mother lived her life being blamed for María's deformity. I'm sure this did not help the bonding process between mother and daughter. María's mother felt the shame and guilt of creating an imperfect child. This usually causes an insurmountable rift between parent and child.
>
> María's illness must have caused her great pain. People in her situation struggle daily to do the most routine tasks that able-bodied people take for granted. Her painting *The Ice Cream Cart* (p. 20), says it all. I look at the boy—happy, carefree, munching on his treat. I see the little girl behind the cart reaching with great effort to get some of the sweetness of life. A crutch is on the floor in the foreground. How telling!

Maria Bonnett is right: it is telling, and it is one of the reasons I love María Blanchard's later work more than the cubist paintings she produced in her middle period. In her earliest and latest paintings, I see narratives, which I personally prefer. However, in the process of putting this book together, I came to appreciate her cubist paintings more than I had previously. I realize she was working to understand the challenges of cubism, to reproduce and go beyond its lessons the way poets may work to create new forms in poetry and in the course of their work come to new discoveries in language and meaning. I am grateful to the Meadows Museum's "Tiny Tour" on YouTube that helped me to better see the museum's *Seated Woman/Femme Assise*. And as Blanchard's cubist work surfaces in recent special exhibits, both in the US and abroad, I am struck by the remark of art critic Maurice Raynal in 1927: "I would not be surprised if in the more or less distant future the historians of Cubism were to consider María Blanchard one of the heroes of this prodigious movement."

I have always loved her grand cubist painting, *Woman with a Fan*, which hangs a floor above Picasso's *Guernica* and next to a Rivera cubist painting in the Reina Sofía Museum in Madrid. This Blanchard painting is a cubist image in a long artistic tradition of studies of women with fans. Her cubist work that references Joan of Arc integrates the words "Sois Sage," or "Behave Yourself," which María heard women say all her life. Her later paintings of mothers and children—the girl with the toothache, the boy with the ice cream cone—really speak to me, too. As my friend Maria Bonnett notes, they are "telling." They have a lot to tell us, and I am keeping my eyes and ears wide open to see and hear what Blanchard's art is telling me, what it can tell us all.

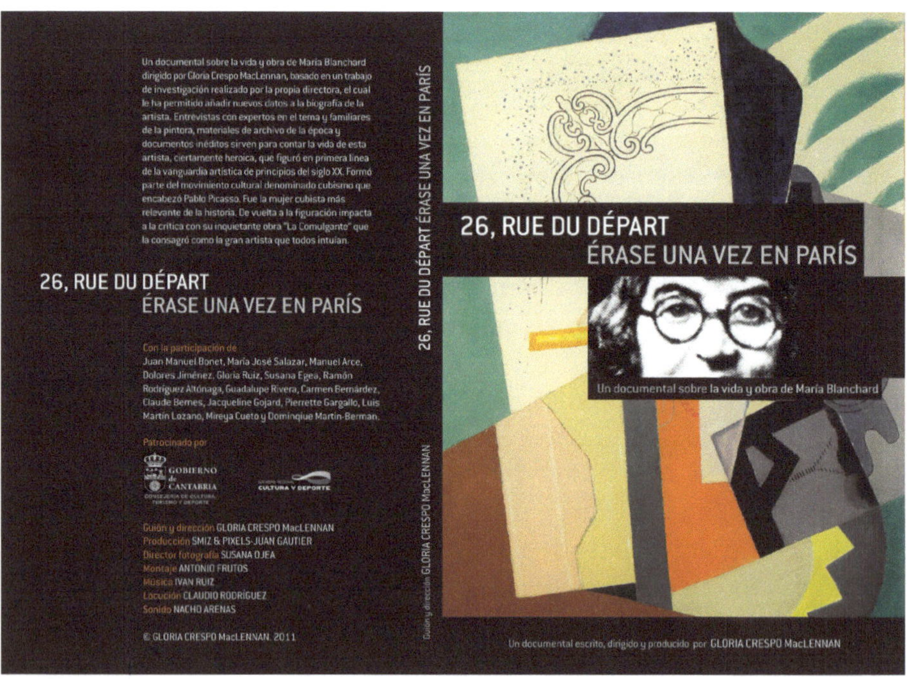

Speaking Even More of María Blanchard

A review of *26, Rue du Départ, Érase una vez en París*[1]

This 2012 hour-long Spanish documentary by Gloria Crespo on the Spanish painter María Blanchard is a typical talking-heads treatment of the artist's life and times, but such heads as are talking here! Spain's top art critics, curators, feminists, and writers, as well as Blanchard's relatives, friends, and relatives of friends, converse here alongside footage of Paris in the early 1900s and images of Blanchard's work. The hope is to rescue this artist's reputation from near oblivion and place her in the pantheon of her contemporaries such as Picasso (who came and walked in her funeral) and Diego Rivera (with whom she once shared a studio).

The film argues that both her gender and her disability worked against her reputation, or even, we might say, were used against her in her own time and in the decades following. Her curator at the Reina Sofía Museum in Madrid, María José Salazar, gives one shocking example of the unfairness Blanchard's work experienced; Blanchard's name was erased from one of her canvases and replaced with that of Juan Gris, her friend but not the author of the work. Diego Rivera's daughter goes on at length (and not with all that much sensitivity) about how Rivera would not become lovers with Blanchard because of her physical deformity, while Salazar discusses with great sensitivity how painful that relationship was for Blanchard. As the poet Lorca noted for himself, "She's a hunchback, you know," and that was usually one of the first things anyone said about Blanchard.[2]

But few have traced how her disability figures in her life and work. The movie does a great job of setting the record straight on both counts. One of the myths about Blanchard is that her disability was caused by her mother's fall from a horse during pregnancy. Among the cast of talking heads is that of Dr. José Ramón Rodriguez Altonaga, seated among x-rays of many spines. Regarding the stories about the causes of her disability, I was glad to hear him say, "No es la verdad . . . [It's not true . . .]."

These things may be caused by a variety of factors, he says. It may be congenital, genetic, but no one is to blame.

Currently, the film is only available in Spain, but I think Americans in general and art lovers world-wide would find it moving and instructive.When I asked Crespo about the possibility of bringing it here, she said that the investment of time and money for subtitling, copyright, and other issues and tasks seem daunting to her right now as she is trying to finish a book on Blanchard. I have noticed that a posting on a Temple University discussion board on issues of disability states that the effect of Blanchard's kyphosis on her work might be a rich area for disability studies.

Having written on Frida Kahlo for years, too, I find both her and Blanchard fascinating and admirable in the excellence they were able to achieve in their chosen endeavor despite debilitating pain and disability. However, the more I come to know about Blanchard, the more I admire how she went it alone and insisted on being the equal—"not the helper of but on the same plane as" the male artists around her, as one of the critics notes of her relationship with Gris. Her stubbornness may have cost her some fame in her own time. (For example, in the depths of her penury, she once bought back her painting *Two Sisters* from a collector because she felt the collector could not appreciate what it meant to her, sister of two sisters that she was.) I am hoping that her stubborn insistence on color, quality, meaning, and effort in art are what we can use today to promote her legacy in our time, and someday soon, in our country as well as her homeland.

---

1. The film is subtitled [translation mine]: A documentary about the life and work of María Blanchard. It is written, directed, and produced by Gloria Crespo.

2. "Elegía a María Blanchard," in *Deep Song and Other Prose,* by Federico Garcia Lorca, edited and translated by Christopher Maurer, New Directions, 1980.

Many Thanks

Two women were especially helpful to me in creating this manuscript. Gloria Crespo reached to me across the ocean from Spain early on to compare notes on what we had each found about Blanchard, and then she sent me her film to view and the art to accompany it. Toward the end, Rosemary Starace read the final manuscript and weighed in with the eye of the artist and words of the writer she is.

Art permissions really bedeviled me, and I am grateful to ekphrastic poet extraordinaire Steve Abbott for early advice, artist Steve Negron for explaining the difference between the image and the photograph of the image, and Anne Lenhart of the Meadows Museum ("The Prado on the Prairie") for her generous assistance in my understanding and use of *Femme Assise.*

I had a lot to learn about disability in its relationship to art and artists. I am especially grateful to Michael Northen, former editor of *Wordgathering*, who suggested many ways I could learn through writing about the issues; and to Maria Bonnett, who taught me what she saw and felt and knew about art and mothers.

Some poem drafts were read by my poetry group, the Eight Elevens, and mostly by the early incarnation of the group, Laura Weldon and Laurie Kincer. One can't have better advice than that from the Ohio Poet of the Year (Laura) and the Writing Specialist of the Cuyahoga County Library (Laurie), both of them are dear to me with talents way beyond what their titles suggest. Actor Robin Johnson requested I write a poem for her and *The New Place*, and I am grateful to her for her recording of that and another poem of mine.

The most thanks to Paul Beauvais, who has read everything I've written and whose responses improve them and me; and who accompanied me back to Spain and was the first to spot the name "María Blanchard" at the Reina Sofía Museum in Madrid, where we found, together, *Woman with a Fan.*

Artwork Credits

[12 / Cover] María Blanchard, *Woman with a Fan / Mujer con abanico*, 1916. Oil on canvas. 63.3 x 38.1 inches (161 x 97 cm). Museo Nacional Centro de Arte Reina Sofía, Madrid, Spain. Public domain.

[17] María Blanchard, *The Communicant / La Comulgante*, 1914. Oil and collage on canvas. 70.8 x 48.8 inches (180 x 124 cm). Museo Nacional Centro de Arte Reina Sofía, Madrid, Spain. Public domain.

[26] María Blanchard, *The Ice Cream Cart / El carrito del helado*, 1925. Oil on canvas. 64 x 39 inches (162 x 99 cm). Centre Pompidou, Paris, France. Public domain. Photo: Art Resource, USA. Used with permission.

[33] María Blanchard, *Seated Woman / Femme Assise*, c. 1917. Oil on canvas. 44 x 30 inches (111. x 77 cm). Meadows Museum, Southern Methodist University, Dallas, Texas. Museum purchase with funds from the Meadows Foundation MM .08.02. Photo: Michael Bodycomb. Used with permission.

[50] *26, Rue du Départ* movie poster. © 2011 Maria Belloso. Used with permission of Gloria Crespo.

Good ekphrastic poetry can stand on its own, but those who enjoy the dual experience of poem and painting can find many of the paintings referred to in this book online. Here, in addition to the English titles, are Spanish titles that do not appear elsewhere in the book.

[15] *Portrait of Regina Barahona / Retrato de Regina Barahona*

[20] *Lady with a Fan / La dama del abanico*

[21] *Oriental Caprice / Capricho Oriental*

[22] *Cubist Still Life / Nature Morte Cubiste*

[24] *Behave Yourself—Joan of Arc / Sois Sage—Juana de Arco*

[23] *Two Sisters / Dos Hermanas*

[28] *Three Portraits / Cabeza de mora, Retrato de joven and Figura de muchacha*

[34] *Child with a Handkerchief (Toothache) / Niña con pañuelo*

About the Author

Diane Kendig has worked as a poet, writer, translator, and teacher, and has authored four poetry collections, most recently, *Prison Terms*. She also co-edited the anthology *In the Company of Russell Atkins*, a tribute to the ninety-three-year-old poet and musician. A recipient of OAC Individual Artist grants and awards from Yaddo, the Fulbright Program, and the National Endowment for the Humanities, Kendig has published poetry and prose in journals such as *J Journal, Wordgathering, Valparaiso Poetry Review*, and *Under the Sun*.

As an undergraduate, Kendig studied English and Spanish and lived a year in Segovia, Spain. She began her college teaching career at Cleveland State, then taught at the University of Findlay for eighteen years, founding its creative writing program, including a prison writing program. She taught translation at Central American University in Managua, Nicaragua, after publication of her collection of Nicaraguan poet translations, *And a Pencil to Write Your Name*.

After living ten years in the Boston area, Kendig moved home to retire in Canton, Ohio, to be with her father, who died in 2019. She bought the house he built himself when he returned from WWII. There she is writing again, alongside her husband, Paul Beauvais, and her Scottie, Robbie Burns Beaudig, and she curates a web blog with four thousand subscribers for the Cuyahoga County Public Library.

dianekendig.com
dianekendig.blogspot.com

SHANTI ARTS

NATURE ▪ ART ▪ SPIRIT

Please visit us online
to browse our entire book catalog,
including poetry collections and fiction,
books on travel, nature, healing, art,
photography, and more.

Also take a look at our highly
regarded art and literary journal,
Still Point Arts Quarterly, which
may be downloaded for free.

www.shantiarts.com

www.ingramcontent.com/pod-product-compliance
Lightning Source LLC
LaVergne TN
LVHW052309100826
845147LV00006B/713

* 9 7 8 1 9 5 1 6 5 1 8 5 5 *